Obama Praises
THE "KOREAN
EDUCATION FERVOR"
Should We Emulate It?

JU-CHUN CHAI

ISBN: 1496193474
ISBN 13: 9781496193476

juchunchai@naver.com

Dedicated to the 972,214 soldiers from seventeen nations who, during the Korean War, fought for and laid the foundation for what Korea has achieved today. Special recognition to the USAID University of Minnesota–Seoul University Program, which rekindled the Korean fervor for education.

TABLE OF CONTENTS

Summary

Korea suffered for thirty-five years (1910–1945) under harsh Japanese colonial economic exploitation and ethnic persecution, and before it could begin to recover, the Korean War broke out (1950–1953). More than 2.6 million soldiers from twenty nations on six continents were involved; the war ended with more than one million civilian and military deaths.

In 1945, under Japanese colonial rule, the Korean literacy rate was 22 percent and per capita gross domestic product (GDP) was $320. In 2012, the literacy rate and per capita GDP increased to 98 percent and $22,590, respectively.

Korea's economic and social conditions after the Korean War were best described by one of my economics professors at the University of Minnesota when he returned from a US government assignment to evaluate economic conditions: "Korea is hopeless." One Korean student asked, "What can we do?" The professor replied in jest, "Suicide." No economist studying Korea's conditions at the time could have expressed the country's war-torn suffering better.

After the war the US government and many private organizations gave Korea large amounts of urgently needed relief goods, such as food and clothing. But in retrospect, the best help was from the US Agency for International Development's (USAID) University of Minnesota–Seoul University Program.

The program sought to improve the quality of the Seoul University teaching staff—especially in agriculture, science, technology, engineering, and medicine—by sending more than two hundred faculty members to the University of Minnesota every year for their graduate work.

This unnoticed USAID program made Seoul University the most prestigious institution in Korea and rekindled Korean educational fervor, leading to what Korea is today.

Indeed, the United States has saved Korea twice since 1945: once by ending the humiliating Japanese colonial rule by winning the Second World War, and five years later by halting North Korea's military invasion, giving us opportunities to become what South Korea is today.

Today, fifteen-year-old Korean students rank first in reading, math, and science (OECD PISA2009 Data

Base), and sixth in the world with regard to sending students beyond secondary education. According to the International Monetary Fund (IMF), the per capita GDP for 2012 was the United States $51,704 (sixth) and Korea $31,571 (twenty-sixth). In 2012 the disposable wage income (take-home pay for a full-time worker) among Organization for Economic Co-operation and Development (OECD) member nations was the United States $42,052 (first) and Korea $31,051 (ninth).

While improving their education and the economy, Koreans did not neglect the arts and sporting events. In the 2012 Olympics they took home thirteen gold medals, fifth among the nations. In terms of population, Korea had one gold medal for every 1.7 million people; the United States, one for every 3.0 million; and Japan, one for every 3.6 million.

President Barack Obama often praised the Korean fervor for education in encouraging elementary and secondary school performance, particularly in math and science.

He said, "If they can do that in South Korea, we can do it right here in the United States of America." Since his visit to Seoul in 2009, President Obama has talked about "the education fervor that contributed to South Korea's rapid economic development in recent decades, and has deplored underperformance of

American students, especially in math and science. In South Korea, teachers are known as nation builders. That's how they're described. Here in America, it's time we treat the people who educate our children with the same level of respect."[1]

Statistics show that American elementary and secondary school performance lags behind other countries, and that money has failed to improve student performance. But when statistics are broken down by race, they show a different picture. White and Asian students in the United States are generally the best-performing students in the world. Indeed, the 2010 census report on college graduate rate and household income data reveals: Asian Americans, 52 percent with college degree, $75,027 household income; whites, 30 percent with college degree, $62,545 household income; blacks, 20 percent with college degree, $38,409 household income; Latinos, 14 percent with college degree, $39,730 household income. All statistical evidence shows education, especially in science and technology, is highly correlated with the wealth of a nation—as well as with the wealth of ethnic groups and individuals.

Respect for teachers is an age-old aspect of East Asian culture, as President Obama observed. Although the old culture is fading, teachers still are respected and well

1   "Obama Lauds S. Korea's Education System," *Korea Herald*, February 9, 2011.

treated. The pay level of the American teacher is slightly below the US average income. The Korean teacher's pay is more than twice the Korean average income.

Based on statistical evidence, there is nothing really wrong with the American education system; the problem is concentrated in low-income, inner-city public schools. The public education system's efforts to resolve the problem by spending more money per student—as in Washington, DC—has not yet achieved the desired result, frustrating everyone in the nation, including the commander in chief. What, then, should Americans do if money does not resolve the problem?

MORE PARENTAL INVOLVEMENT

Korean "tiger moms" are totally dedicated to their children's education. They take great pleasure in the process as well as pride in how well their children perform in school. They are more involved than the average American parent (excepting Asian American parents). Former Delaware Lt. Governor S. B. Woo said, "Many Asian Americans live for their children, sacrificing everything to pay phenomenal tuition at these private schools They at the same time, are very much aware that their kids have to cross much higher admission bar." http://www.bloomberg.com/news/2012-02/harvard-targeted-in-u-s-asian-american

Emulating the Asian culture of more parental involvement in education may be one way to change the course of underperforming schoolchildren both in the United States and around the world. More money and government regulation have not worked for decades in the United States.

MORE USE OF IT

Much technology was invented and developed in the United States, and Koreans are making the best use of it at school and elsewhere. Korean children topped the PISA digital literacy test in 2009. Every school in Korea has high-speed Internet, digital textbooks, and a Cyber Home Learning System, which is an online program designed to help students with after-school learning. Studies have shown that technology can help all children learn faster and develop deeper basic academic skills.

The use of IT is not limited to education, however. The government, businesses, banking, hospitals, airports, and other industries all take advantage of technology for efficiency. For example, I used to wait for ten to twenty minutes for my prescription drugs; now my wait time is one or two minutes, saving time, money, and frustration.

1

WHAT'S WRONG WITH US K–12 EDUCATION?

WHAT'S KOREA DOING RIGHT?

It has been said that figures never lie, but a liar can figure. Figures in statistics are seldom exact and are not meant to be; however, a rough figure is better than a precisely wrong number. Statistical numbers differ by how and who collected them.

President Truman expressed his frustration with economist's conflicting views and joked, "All my economists say, 'on one hand...on the other' give me a one-handed economist." So far, no president found a one-handed economist, yet.

The figures below, compiled by OECD, definitely show that Korean, Finnish, and Japanese children are among the best in reading, math, and science.

TABLE 1. EDUCATION ACHIEVEMENT TESTS, FIFTEEN-YEAR-OLDS ON READING, MATH, AND SCIENCE, BY SELECTED COUNTRY, 2009

Country	Ranking	Reading	Math	Science
S. Korea	1	539	546	554
Finland	2	536	541	539
Japan	5	520	527	529
United States	14	500	501	506
UK	20	491	494	499

Source: OECD PISA 2009 database; ranking is just within OECD countries. http://the guardian.com/news/datablog/2010/dec/07/world-education.

Visiting education specialists and native English teachers in Korea are often concerned about the health effects of Korean children sleeping only about five hours a day, doing nothing else but sitting and memorizing books. However, the following statistics on sports and longevity show that most Koreans do more than just sitting and studying. Koreans win more Olympic gold medals in terms of the population than Japan, China, or the United States, and they live longer than many other nationalities, including Chinese and Americans.

TABLE 2. AVERAGE WAGE, OLYMPIC GOLD MEDALS, AND
LONGEVITY, BY SELECTED COUNTRY, 2012

Country	Average wage ($)	Olympic gold	Longevity (years)
United States	42,050	46	79.8
S. Korea	31,051	13	81.0
Japan	27,763	8	82.6

*Sources: Average wage, 2011, http://stats.oecd.org/index.aspx;
Olympic gold medal count, medal standings, BBC retrieved February
24, 2014; Longevity, WHO, 2013.*

What Korea is doing right in education and for living standards is notable, but the speed at which Korea changed from a war-torn, downtrodden nation to what is its now (fifty years later) is a model for individuals and nations.

I fully agree with President Obama that American elementary and secondary students can improve dramatically, can, in fact, be far better than Korean children because American children do not have to spend half of their study time and the largest portion of private education money to learn English at expensive private language schools. Korean families, who earn much less than what an American family earns, spend $200 to $500 a month for each of their children—from preschool to college—to attend private English language schools taught by American,

British, Canadian, Australian, Indian, South African, and Filipino teachers.

I also agree with President Obama's emphasis on math, science, and technology education that leads to the wealth of nations, all ethnicities, and all individuals, as shown statistically in Chapter 2. This idea is not new. For example, the concept of the land-grant university—a publicly funded institution of higher education that began in the United States in 1860—emphasized agricultural and technical education that required a mastery of math and science.

Right now, the world is facing a dire shortage of science, technology, and skill workers in the midst of an increasing number of college graduates without jobs. This supply-and-demand mismatch in the labor market is a sad commentary more visible in educationally advanced nations such as the United States, Japan, Korea, and Europe.

KOREA'S ACHILLES HEEL

Korean and Japanese students spend more money and time per person learning English than any other subject, including math and science, but are last in the world in English speaking and writing. As noted in *Time* magazine ("Loving English—but Not Well: The Japanese Still Take Poorly to the World's No. 2

Language," January 8, 1989, p. 31): Japanese Prime Minister Takeshita, a former English teacher, addressed the National Press Club in Washington, DC. He used a translator and quipped, "Pity my students; they had to suffer through my lessons without benefit of a translator." "Takeshita's problem is not unique in Japan; in fact, it is endemic." Koreans and Japanese suffer most because their two languages are very similar. It seems that Chinese, South East Asians, East Indians, Arabs, Africans, and South Americans have fewer problems mastering English.

American students do not have to spend so much time and money just to learn English. Thus, they and the rest of the world can devote more time and money to other subjects, including all-important math and science, and can easily do better than Korean and Japanese students in all subjects as well as in future individual income, which is related to the attainment of education.

MONEY FAILED TO IMPROVE US K-12 PUBLIC SCHOOL EDUCATION

American families and their government together spend more money than their Korean counterparts for preschool through twelfth-grade education. Then what went wrong with American elementary and secondary education with a huge advantage in funding? Many outstanding American educators are voicing their concerns as well as possible solutions.

Statistics reveal that far too many American public schools are failing the students, teachers, and parents, particularly inner-city schools. Former Secretary of Education William J. Bennett said, "After spending $118 billion since 1965 on Title I, the federal government's largest K–12 program, evaluations conclude that the program has been unable to lift the academic level of poor students."[1]

American Achievement in International Perspective, from the Thomas B. Fordham Institute (March 15, 2011), states that "the picture changes when low achievers, Blacks and Hispanics, in the U.S. are broken out by race. White and Asian students in the United States are generally among the best-performing pupils in the world; Black and Hispanic students in the U.S. have very high rates of low achievement. Black and Hispanic students do outperform their counterparts in all African and Hispanic countries."

The 2010 census shows that among the four American racial groups, Asians had the highest educational attainment (52 percent college degree) and household income ($75,027); followed by whites (30 percent, $62,505); blacks (20 percent, $38,409); and Hispanics (14 percent, $39,730). The average Hispanic income is higher than the average black income because of

---

1   William J. Bennett, "20 Troubling Facts about American Education," Catholic Education Research Center, 2012.

larger family size—and therefore more earners in the household (2.6 vs. 3.2).

Thus, the US education problem is concentrated in some underprivileged, low-income black and Hispanic groups. All other information so far indicates that the rest of the population is doing fine academically. The earlier mentioned fact that Asian Americans have a much higher rate of college graduation than their peers in Korea, Japan, China, and India implies that there is perhaps nothing really wrong with the US K–12 education system.

We have seen that many years of more funding for students and teachers, fewer students per class, more administrative support staff, and new regulations, along with other educational efforts to solve the achievement gap, have not produced the desired results, disappointing and puzzling everyone.

Total expenditures per student in fall enrollment in public elementary and secondary schools, in constant 2011–12 dollars, increased by 20 percent from 1999–2000 ($9,292) to 2009–10 ($11,184) (Public School Expenditures, The Condition of Education-Elementary and Secondary Education-Finance-Public. http://nces.ed.gov/programs/coe/indicator).

Bennett also cited in "20 Troubling Facts about American Education" that "Average per-pupil spending in U.S. public school rose 212% from 1960 to 1995 in real dollars. In 1960, for every U.S. public teacher there were approximately 26 students enrolled in the school class. In 1995, there were 17. In 1994, fewer than 50% of the personnel employed by U.S. public schools were teachers. The average salary of U.S. teachers rose 45% in real dollars from 1960 to 1995."

All statistical evidence so far shows that all efforts by the government have rather negative results concerning student achievement. A statistical correlation does not necessarily indicate the root cause, but at least we know that government efforts have not worked as hoped. Now what? A plausible solution could be a cultural one, such as more family involvement, not more government funding, in K-12 education. President Obama is coming up with a suggestion after a few visits to Korea, during which he extolled the Korean fervor for education.

From 1945 to 1948 the American military administration took over Korea, replacing the defeated Japanese colonial government. A US Army general served as governor (president), and a US Army captain served as secretary of education, and transplanted the US education system to Korea. Since then, both the United States and Korea have had some minor changes in their education systems, but they are about the same.

The major difference is Korea spends much more money in relation to national income and per household income on education than the United States, indicating that Koreans are placing education first and sacrificing national and family needs. However, on an absolute monetary basis, the United States spends much more money than Korea does. The average US public schools compared to Korean schools have fewer students per teacher and have far more administrative and support staff, and generally better school facilities. The statistically supported argument advanced by former Secretary of Education Bennett that more school spending and use of resources did little to improve the K–12 public school student achievement is also applicable across the nation and region at a given time.

According to a *Washington Post* article, "The Washington D.C. School District spends $12,979 per student per year. This is the third highest level of funding per student out of the 100 school districts in the U.S. However, these schools are ranked last in the amount of funding spent on teachers and instruction, and first on the amount spent on administration.

The school district has produced academic results that are lower than the national average. In reading and math, the district's students scored the lowest among 11 major school districts even when the poor children are compared with other poor children. 33% of poor fourth graders in the U.S. lack basic skills in math, but in Washington D. C. it's 62%" (Michelle Singletary, "The Color of Money: Getting Through College These Days Requires a Degree in Thrift," *Washington Post*, October 22, 2009, p. 20A).

In contrast, private American primary and secondary schools are doing just fine. I served as a guardian for some Korean students attending a private military academy in Virginia, and the school did a fine job of instilling discipline in each student, even better than did their parents in Korea. Once the school called to inform me that my ward had gotten into a fight with another student, and asked me to warn him not to repeat the misbehavior. The graduate is now a veterinarian.

Under the system of socialized primary education, many traditional family responsibilities, such as children's character building and discipline, are being transferred to the schools under the assumption that teachers will take on parental responsibilities. But teachers can't properly manage this job because their primary responsibility is teaching assigned subjects; they do not have extra time for teaching manners and discipline.

Education and self-discipline are challenging for both the rich and the poor. Euclid (330–260 BC) said to the king he taught, "There is no royal road to Geometry." Greeks were known for their high level of self-discipline, as demonstrated by the Spartan warriors. Education and discipline were the building blocks of the ancient Greek empire. On the other hand, the lack of financial discipline in modern Greece is taking the country through a Greek tragedy—high government and individual debt, high youth unemployment, and frequent street riots by frustrated and unhappy citizens. Other financially irresponsible and undisciplined nations are going through the same tragedy.

I found a surprisingly good definition of self-discipline on a blog, rather appropriately named thespartanwarrior.com, that calls self-discipline "the way to turn your intention to reality. Self-discipline is the way to transform your weakness into strength. Without discipline, even when you know what you want, you're unable to achieve it. Without discipline, even though you know what you don't want, you're unable to avoid it.

"Self-discipline is essential to living life on your own terms. It takes effort, it takes determination, it takes sacrifice, yet it is not a punishment. Rather, it is a fulfillment, the means to reaching your highest and best possibilities.

"How do you get self-discipline? You already have it. It involves nothing more than controlling your own actions, and you've been doing that since you were a child. To discipline yourself, you simply must decide to do it. The powerful tool of self-discipline is yours to use whenever you're ready to live life on your terms."

Early parental infusion of self-discipline is the foundation for educational attainment. The school and government are not equipped to handle this preschool family responsibility. For socialized education to succeed, the family must do their part in their children's early education. Children's education should be a joint venture between the family's disciplinary education and the school's academic education.

Similar views were expressed by Lennerd B. in "U. S. Education Spending & Performance vs. the World." "The first and most important teacher every child has is her/his parent. The kids in private schools generally have benefitted from the superior parenting that money helps to provide, that is, opportunities for exploration, travel, music, dance, golf, tennis lessons, etc. A person's outlook is mostly formed by the time they are five years old".

"Those so called 'disadvantages' you're citing that private schools have are more than made up for by the counterweight of parental education involvement, and the esteem with which such parents view the education of their kids. The schools and their teachers have a far easier lift than a school and a teacher have in the ghetto. I know, I have taught in both Los Angeles public schools where almost all parents of the kids are 1st generation immigrants and in private schools where the kids were the children and grandchildren of Nobel Prize winning scientists".

"Another problem is generational education and financial cycle of poverty found in socialized education countries including the U.S."

"Parents, not the school teachers, transmit the intellectual, social, and cultural mixes which cannot be easily changed. One American licensed social worker said when parents are stable, kids are stable."

JanDo: "Yes, private schools here in America have been shown to outperform public schools even though they are in 'disadvantaged' with significantly lower teacher salaries, lower degree of teacher education, and higher teacher turnover rates. Also, private schools here find a way to spend 1/3 to almost 1/2 of the amount that public schools do per student. I wouldn't blame private schools for our education problems. I would look to them for solutions."

Martin S.: "The decline started when the depth of education was implemented. Cost went up and results went down. This is what happens when you try to implement the socialist idea that everyone has to be equal. It is impossible to make everyone equal to the brightness so we take the brightness and dumb them down. Results are all are equally mediocre. It costs a lot of money to do this".

However, America still has one bright spot in education: its colleges and universities. They are among the best in the world: forty of the top one hundred educational institutions in the world are American, attracting an increasing number of foreign students, especially from China, India, and Korea. Those three Asian countries contribute nearly 50 percent of all foreign students to the United States.

WHAT CAN PEOPLE LEARN FROM KOREA?

Many people, especially foreign visitors, mention that Korean schools and private "cram institutes" are too intense, that parental and social pressures on children are too great. But, by and large, the current generation of children has a much better overall social and economic environment than my generation, which suffered under the unbearable Japanese colonial rule during World War II and then endured the Korean War. These unending miseries actually served as a "wake-up call" from a hopeless to a hopeful nation. Despite the current imperfections of the Korean education approach, there are a few things people in other cultures can learn from it.

MORE PARENTAL INVOLVEMENT.

Korean tiger moms are fully dedicated to their children's education—to the point of overdoing it. Their pleasure and social standing among their peers depend on how well their kids are doing in school.

Normally, the father is in charge of financial support and the mother is in charge of raising children and teaching proper manners and discipline. Parents teach music, sports, arts, and hobbies, but do not get involved with school subjects; they leave that part to professional teachers because the content of the school curriculum changes so fast and parents are not equipped to handle the job. Korean parents of all social classes, rich or poor, instill the importance of education from early childhood. They and society recognize the fact that the attainment of education affects personal income and social standing, and that giving good education to children is the best lifetime heritage.

This was not the case one hundred years ago when the Korean "caste system" made it difficult for children to advance beyond their heritage. Now, everyone has an equal opportunity if one has a good education, and everyone, including very poor parents, are trying harder to have their children escape the cycle of "poor education–poor living" endured by their parents due to the caste system.

Unlike American low-income and single-parent families, Korean low-income and single-mother families would be first to get on the education bandwagon. Korean parents move within the country, seeking better school districts; many parents might even move to another country seeking better educational opportunities.

RESPECT FOR TEACHERS.

Traditionally, Koreans are taught to respect their parents and teachers. This tradition has been slowly fading. However, some of my former students still come to see me and pay their respects.

OECD reports indicate that American K–12 teachers spend, on average, 1,080 hours in the classroom each year. OECD average: Primary school, 794 hours; Lower secondary school, 709 hours; Upper secondary school, 653 hours (Catherine Rampell, "Teacher Pay Around the World," *New York Times,* September 9,

2009. http://ecomomix.blogs.nytimes/2009/09/09/teacher-pay-around-the-world).

In the United States a teacher with fifteen years of experience makes a salary that is 90 percent of the GDP per capita as compared to the OECD average of 117 percent, and Korea's 221 percent (the top among OECD countries). Korean teachers' salaries compared to other Korean professionals indicate high esteem for teachers and attract the best college graduates in the country. Korean K–12 teachers have about three months of paid vacation, and college professors have almost four months of paid vacation, while other professions in Korea have a much shorter paid leave.

The *Korea Herald* reports that U.S. President Barack Obama Tuesday called on " the U.S. to benchmark South Korea in rebuilding the country through education reform. In South Korea, teachers are known as 'nation builders,' Obama said during a classroom visit at Tech Boston Academy in the capital city of Massachusetts. "That's how they're described. Here in America, it's time we treated the people who educate our children with the same level of respect. We've got to lift up teachers. We've got to reward good teachers. Also, we have to stop making excuses for bad teachers. Let's also remember that after parents, the biggest impact on a child's success comes from the man or woman at the front of the classroom," he said. "In South Korea, teachers are known as nation builders" ("Obama Lauds S. Korea's Education System," *Korea Herald,* February 9, 2011).

2

EDUCATION CAUSES THE WEALTH OF NATIONS, ETHNICS, AND INDIVIDUALS

In 1776 Adam Smith wrote about the nature and causes of wealth in *The Wealth of Nations.* He pointed out that the improvement in labor productivity through division of labor and specialization leads to wealth.

For labor specialization to be more effective, one needs education and training in science, technology, and onsite skills Two centuries later, empirical evidence shows that education—particularly in science, technology, and production skills—is the major cause of the wealth of nations, as well as of the wealth of ethnic groups and individuals.

Despite being in the minority, Europeans after the sixteenth century colonized and dominated vast areas of Asia, Africa, and America because of their advances in science and technology.

Of the three Hermit Kingdoms of Asia—China, Japan, and Korea—Japan first copied Western science and military arts and easily beat both China and Russia in naval and land war, and then easily colonized Korea without even a fight.

The scientifically and technologically advanced America defeated the Kamigaze fight to the death Japanese military during the Second World War, rescuing China and Korea from the Japanese invasion.

Above historical track records clearly, show that the advances in science and technology through education can make or break a nation and people.

EDUCATION AND NATIONAL INCOME

North and South America are both endowed with different but equally abundant natural resources, and European settlers took them over from the original inhabitants centuries ago.

At the time, South American natives perhaps had more advanced agriculture and engineering—and greater wealth—than their northern counterparts.

Today, the situation is reversed: the North is the strongest economic and military power in the world due to the government's early emphasis on education, land-grant colleges, agriculture (when more than 50 percent of the population was on farms), science and engineering, medicine, and eventually sports, arts, literature, and other aspects of education. Developments in science, engineering, and technology have ripple effects (synergy and multiplier) on agriculture, medicine, sports, arts, and all other aspects of our lives.

Table 3 shows the literacy rate, GDP per capita, and IQ scores of four North and South American countries.

TABLE 3. LITERACY RATE (2012), GDP PER CAPITA, AND IQ SCORES (2013), BY SELECTED COUNTRY

Country	Literacy rate (%)	GDP per capita ($)	IQ scores
US	99	49,695	98
Canada	99	52,219	99
Brazil	87	11,340	87
Mexico	86	9,747	88

Sources: Literacy rate, CIA World Facebook, January 1, 2012; GDP per capita, World Economic Database, IMF, April 1, 2014; IQ scores, Richard Lynn, http://www.photius/rankings_iq_scores_country_ranks.html.

ASIA

India held off Alexander the Great's advances in 300 BC with its fine military tactics and its trained battle elephants that horrified Alexander's horses. The Greek conqueror was also amazed at India's advanced architecture and civil engineering. However, at the end of

British rule in 1947, India's literacy rate was 12 percent. It has now increased to 61 percent, still below the world average, and India is near the bottom of world income.

In contrast, the East Indian ethnic group tops the list of ethnic groups for US household income (2010: $90,525; US average $51,222) through education, especially in science and technology fields.

In 1945, after Japanese colonial rule, the Korean literacy rate was 22 percent, and the per capita GDP was $320, lower than the 2012 Afghanistan literacy rate of 28 percent. Table 4 shows literacy rate, GDP per capita, and IQ score by selected country.

TABLE 4. LITERACY RATE (2012), GDP PER CAPITA, AND IQ SCORES (2013), BY SELECTED COUNTRY

Country	Literacy rate (Rank)	GDP per capita	IQ scores
Asia			
S. Korea	98 (60)	$22,590	106
Mongolia	97 (65)	3,673	101
Vietnam	94 (87)	1,590	94
Philippines	93 (101)	2,587	86
Thailand	93 (102)	5,480	91
China	92 (106)	6,188	100
India	61 (177)	1,489	82
Bangladesh	57 (184)	747	82

Pakistan	55 (189)	1,290	84
Afghanistan	28 (204)	620	84
Africa			
Zimbabwe	91 (115)	788	82
S. Africa	86 (136)	7,508	77
Egypt	72 (160)	3,187	81
Algeria	70 (163)	5,404	83
Morocco	56 (186)	2,902	84
Ethiopia	43 (195)	470	69
Niger	29 (203)	383	69
Middle East			
Kuwait	93 (95)	51,497	86
Jordan	93 (100)	4,945	84
Lebanon	87 (131)	9,775	82
Turkey	87 (132)	10,666	90
Saudi Arabia	87 (135)	25,136	84
Syria	80 (146)	3,289	83
Iraq	78 (149)	6,455	87
Iran	77 (151)	6,816	84
Yemen	61 (174)	1,494	85

Sources: Literacy rate: CIA World Facebook, January 1, 2012; GDP per capita: World Economic Database, IMF, April 1, 2014; IQ scores: Richard Lynn, http://www.photius/rankings_iq_scores_country_ranks.html

The literacy rates and per capita income of a country are closely associated. With a few exception—such as the oil-rich countries of Kuwait and Saudi

Arabia—the former colonies of Europe, particularly those colonized by Great Britain and Spain, have high levels of illiteracy and poverty even years after they were freed from their colonial yokes.

Among the Middle Eastern nations, Kuwait and Saudi Arabia stand out in terms of per capita income because European chemists found ways to convert the raw materials beneath their lands into the "black gold" essential to many must-have commodities.

Table 5 shows the list of the top fifteen countries by average wage. The data represent full-time average annual gross wages and salaries of entire economy of selected OECD member countries. The average wage is a measure of the financial well-being of a country's inhabitants.

TABLE 5. TOP 15 AVERAGE WAGE COUNTRIES, 2011

1	US	$42,052
2	Ireland	41,170
3	Luxembourg	37,997
4	Switzerland	35,471
5	Australia	34,952
6	UK	33,513
7	Canada	32,662

8	Norway	32,620
9	S. Korea	31,051
10	Netherlands	29,269
11	Austria	29,008
12	Sweden	28,301
13	Denmark	27,979
14	Japan	27,763
15	France	27,452

Source: Average wage, 2009, http://stats.oecd.org/index.aspx.

The OECD provided information on the percentage of residents aged twenty-five to sixty-four with a tertiary education for each of its thirty-four member countries.

TABLE 6. TEN MOST COLLEGE-EDUCATED COUNTRIES, 2009

Canada	51%
Israel	46
Japan	45
United States	42
New Zealand	41
S. Korea	40
UK	38

Finland	38
Australia	38
Ireland	37

Source: Michael B. Sauter and Alexander E. M. Hess, 24/7 Wall St., Sept 24, 2012. http://finance.yahoo.com/news/the-most-educated-country-in-the-world.htm.

Private spending on education relative to public spending is much larger in the countries with the highest rates of tertiary education. The OECD average private spending is 16 percent: the US average is 28 percent, and the Korean average is more than 40 percent. In Korea, the largest portion of private education spending is on private English lessons (preschool to college), followed by math (secondary school), music/arts and sports (college age).

EDUCATION AND ETHNIC INCOME

Statistical evidence shows that the income of individual and ethnic groups is also highly correlated with the level of educational attainment.

TABLE 7. COLLEGE DEGREE AND INCOME, BY US ETHNIC GROUP, 2003 AND 2010

Ethnic group	College degree (%)		Income ($)	
	2003	2010	2003	2010
Asian	51	52	42,246	75,027
White	28	30	36,915	62,545
Black	18	20	21,423	38,409
Latino	12	14	23,431	39,730

Source: US Dept. of Commerce, Economics and Statistical Administration, Bureau of the Census, Statistical Abstract of the Unites States, Education, Income, Expenditures, Poverty and Wealth, Annual.

Asian Americans constitute 4 to 5 percent of the American population and have been subjected to all sorts of racial discrimination and persecution. The first-generation Asian immigrants worked on railroad construction or were domestic help or farmhands, the bottom of the social ladder. They stepped up to the next rung by farming and running small businesses such as eateries and laundries. However, they sent their children to the best schools their income permitted, hoping that their educated children would truly experience America as advertised—a land of opportunity and freedom for all, aspirations they had never had for themselves.

Despite a higher admissions bar to undergraduate institutions for Asian students, Asian Americans persevered and are now overrepresented at Harvard (16–18 percent) and Princeton (14–17 percent).

Ironically, persecuted ethnic groups such as Jews in Europe, Asians in America, and Koreans under the Japanese often found their escape route in education, and ended up doing better than the groups who persecuted them. On the other hand, US government welfare programs, though well intended, turned the once brave and proud American Indians into a broken ethnic group: lowest in education and income, and highest in various crimes and health problems at the 360 Indian reservations across the country.

Jews suffered the worst and longest persecution in written history, but through education they moved ahead of all ethnic groups, as evident in the following Nobel Prize winner statistics. (Bear in mind that Jews constitute 0.2 percent of the world's population and 2 percent of the US population.)

TABLE 8. JEWISH NOBEL PRIZE WINNERS, PERCENT OF ALL INDIVIDUAL RECIPIENTS, BY CATEGORY

Category	World	US
Chemistry	22%	33%
Economics	39	50
Literature	12	27
Peace	9	10

| Physics | 26 | 37 |
| Physiology or Medicine | 27 | 40 |

Source: Jewish Nobel Prize Winners http://www.info.org.

It is noted that Jewish Nobel Prize winners are more heavily concentrated in subjects related to science, medicine, and economics.

EDUCATION AND INDIVIDUAL INCOME

The Georgetown University Center on Education and the Workforce examined just what a college degree is worth in lifetime earnings. The data show that a college degree is key to economic opportunities, conferring substantially higher earnings on those with that credential than those without. Moreover, the difference in earning between those who go to college and those who don't is growing—meaning that a college education is more important than ever.

TABLE 9. EARNINGS AND UNEMPLOYMENT RATES BY
EDUCATIONAL ATTAINMENT, 2012

Education attained	Unemployment rate	Median weekly earnings
Doctoral Degree	2.5%	$1,624
Professional Degree	2.1	1,735
Master's Degree	3.5	1,300
Bachelor's Degree	4.5	1,066

Associate's Degree	6.2	785
Some College	7.7	727
High School	8.3	652
Less than High School	12.4	471

Sources: Anthony P. Carnevale, Stephen J. Rose, and Ban Cheah, The College Payoff, Georgetown University, Center on Education and the Workforce; US Bureau of Labor Statistics, Current Population Survey, 2012.

TABLE 10. LIFETIME (40 YEARS) EARNING (2009 DOLLARS), BY EDUCATIONAL ATTAINMENT

Educational attainment	Lifetime earning
Professional Degree	3,648,000
Doctoral Degree	3,252,000
Master's Degree	2,671,000
Bachelor's Degree	2,268,000
Associate's Degree	1,727,000
Some College	1,547,000
High School	1,304,000
Less than High School	973,000

Sources: Anthony P. Carnevale, Stephen J. Rose, and Ban Cheah, The College Payoff, Georgetown University, Center on Education and the Workforce; US Bureau of Labor Statistics, Current Population Survey, 2012.

All statistical evidence shows that more education leads to more earning and a lower unemployment rate. There are, however, significant variations in individual cases due to factors such as age, gender, race/ethnicity, occupation, and perhaps individual fortune or misfortune.

For a humorous example, consider the American economics professor who gave a lecture on the statistical correlation between education and income at a college in South America. After the lecture, one of the students asked the professor, "How come you are not rich with all that education?"

A great number of the world's inventions were created by unschooled individuals. Thomas Edison, for example, had only three months of formal schooling before dropping out and then being taught at home by his mother, but he had as many as 1,093 inventions.

The mother of George Eastman (the founder of Kodak) took in boarders to survive and to pay for George's schooling. The young George left school early and started inventing and working; he became one of the richest people of his time and donated his fortune to colleges and universities at home and abroad.

On a national level, the type and amount of natural resources affect the income level of each country. Since the human race started farming after the Ice Age around 12,000 years ago, to the development of science and technology after the Middle Ages, farmland was the most important natural resource and the most important input for production and income source.

Since the development of science and technology—a result of education—we can convert useless and even harmful natural resources to very useful natural resources. Likewise, we can also convert, through education, less productive human resource to more productive human resource in terms of earning power.

The best example is oil. Until chemists found ways to convert raw oil to varieties of fuel and chemicals, oil was good only for making farmland useless. It was called a "black nuisance" then; now we call it "black gold" and can't live without it.

SUPPLY- AND DEMAND-MISMATCH IN EDUCATION

Many educationally advanced nations are facing a worsening mismatch in supply and demand for skilled talents while suffering increasing numbers of unemployed college graduates. The OECD reports that "between 2000 and 2010, the percentage of South Koreans with a college education or more rose from 24% to 40%. In addition to being well educated, many residents also invested considerable amounts toward their schooling".

"Despite the investment, education does not appear to have a measurable impact on job seekers. The unemployment rate in 2010 for those with a tertiary degree was 3.3%—low relative to the OECD average of 4.7%, but not much lower than the 3.7% rate for all workers in the country."

The OECD report also quotes a *Wall Street Journal* article that "recent university graduates in Japan have struggled to find work, with 15% of those graduating in the spring of 2012 neither employed nor enrolled in further education as of August."

The large numbers of unemployed college graduates are nothing new for Japan and Korea. Traditional emphasis on liberal arts (when anyone who could read and write could get a job fifty years ago) tends to produce too many idle intellectuals and not enough technicians and highly skilled workers. To fill the skilled labor gaps, Korean businesses are hiring large numbers of overseas skilled workers at internationally competitive wages with extra stipends, indicating that Korean colleges and the government are not doing their jobs.

The Korean and Japanese call unemployed college graduates "high-class drifters." The education system is dumping them on the street year after year while employers are having a difficult time finding qualified employees at home and overseas.

This isn't happening solely in Asia. "Manpower Group surveyed nearly 40,000 employers in 42 countries, including more than 1,000 U.S. employers. Some 39% of U.S. employers continue to have difficulty finding people with the right skills—the highest since the start of the recession."

"Here are the top 10 shortage jobs:

1. Skilled traders (good with math and tech knowledge)

2. Sales reps (with tech knowledge)

3. Drivers

4. IT staff

5. Accounting and Finance

6. Engineering

7. Technicians

8. Management/Exec

9. Mechanics

10. Teachers (math and science)

"Globally, the three most challenging areas are skilled traders, engineers, and sales representatives with tech knowledge.

"Employers are having the most difficulty in Japan (85%), Brazil (68%), India (61%), Turkey (58%) and Hong Kong (58%)."[2]

Former Secretary of Education Bennett points out that the root of the imbalance in the supply-and-demand situation is US colleges. His argument is also applicable globally. "He would prefer to see the United States emulate countries like Germany, where most young people are tracked into vocational training, and he wants more Americans who do go to college to study science, technology, engineering and mathematics rather than what he calls "irrelevant material."[3]

Globally, as more employers embrace the advanced high-tech business model, more skilled technicians will be needed. The education system must adjust to meet the constantly changing demand for skilled labor—a global challenge for tertiary education. To do this, another land-grant college approach may be needed whereby the three relevant sectors—the

---

2 "Survey Finds Skill Talent Shortages Continue Both in U. S. and Globally," GlobalHR, HR News and Trends. http://www.tknt.com/2013/o5/29/survey-finds-skilled-talent-shortages-continue-b.

3 Andrew Delbanco, "Illiberal Arts," *New York Times Book Review* June 21, 2013, p. 22.

government, education, and the business community—closely communicate and collaborate to reduce the global human resource supply-and-demand imbalance sector by sector.

Korean Education Fervor: History and Culture

IN THE BEGINNING

Chinese symbols, which originated about eight thousand years ago, are the oldest and most widely adopted writing system in the world. They are the common writing system in China, Korea, Japan, and Vietnam, as well as for many other ethnic groups. They facilitated a sharing of culture among the largest group of nations in history until the Latin alphabet replaced Chinese symbols as the overall global writing system, mostly due to the spread of English.

Functional literacy requires knowledge of about three thousand Chinese characters. Lessons begin around age three and go on through the late teens to achieve proficiency. One can express thoughts in fewer Chinese symbols than phonetic Korean, Japanese, or English alphabets because of their pictorial nature.

Chinese symbols therefore facilitate speed-reading and writing space by taking fewer characters to express a subject or thought. As an illustration, consider the following words: mountain (山), river (川), farmland (田).

Two of the most famous Chinese teachers and philosophers are Confucius (551–479 BC) and Mencius (372–289 BC). Both were raised by poor single mothers. Mencius's mother is often held up as an exemplary figure in Asian culture—the original Asian tiger mom. She relocated three times before finding a residence that she felt was right for her child's upbringing. First they lived by a cemetery, where the mother found her son imitating the paid mourners in funeral processions, a custom still observed in some parts of Asia. She decided to move. The next house was near a market in town. There the boy began to imitate the cries of hawkers, so the mother moved to a house next to a school. Inspired by the scholars and students, Mencius began to study. His mother decided to remain, and Mencius became a scholar.

Korean mothers still follow this tradition by moving to where there is a better school for their children, often paying a much higher price for housing, and even going so far as to take the children to the United States while the husband works in Korea to pay expensive American private tuition. The Korean name for such fathers is "goose dads" because of the need to fly back and forth to see his family. Knowing the stress placed on marriage and the household budget, this is an extremely high risk taken for a prestigious American education. In terms of respective population size, Koreans send their students to American universities more than twenty-six times as often as the Chinese and sixteen times as often as the Indians.

For those students who remain in the country, the National College Entrance Examination is held on a nationally observed day. It is the most important day in a student's life because the exam score determines what school the student can attend, which eventually leads to both social standing and economic status. Koreans understandably take it very seriously. All activities in the country grind to a halt on that day. Offices open late to clear the traffic for students, planes are not allowed to fly over the test sites, and parents and grandparents go to temples and other religious sites to pray while children take the exams. The country turns into a madhouse that no other nation can match. I believe even Confucius and Mencius would regard this with some amusement.

Confucius and Mencius, contrary to what some Westerners think, were not religious leaders. Once a student asked Confucius about life after death, and Confucius replied, "How do I know about life after death? I do not even know enough about the present life." Confucius, who once served as a king's minister, was asked what are the three most important things about governing people?. He said these were food to live, an army to protect the nation, and—most important of all—trust between the ruler and the ruled. Both Confucius and Mencius emphasized education, regarding learning as a lifelong endeavor and as life itself.

In traditional Korean culture, the mother assumes the all-out support of a child's education. Korean mothers, however, do not get directly involved with teaching the reading and writing of English at home, as some American parents do, because Korean reading and writing can be mastered in a day. In fact, I taught my American roommate how to read and write Korean in four hours. Of course, he did not know the meaning of the words.

Based on my observations and Korean historical evidence, single mothers often do a better job of raising and educating children. Mothers often hang all their hopes on their children and become tiger moms. Children respond to the loving and devoted mother by not disappointing her hopes and expectations. Among my classmates, my most successful friends were those raised by poor single moms. These include a Korean ambassador to the United Nations whose mother was a seamstress in a poor neighborhood; a CEO of a major Japanese firm whose mother had a small retail shop; and two real estate tycoons whose mother had a lunchroom for ox-cart drivers in order to earn enough money to send her two children to college—one became a college dean, and the other one, my classmate, owns a publishing house. Both of them made money in real estate on the side. President Obama was also raised by a single mother, and look how well he has done!

Lino Graglia, a University of Texas law professor, has suggested that blacks and Hispanics are falling behind in education because they are increasingly raised in single-parent families (Lino Graglia, "Decries Single Motherhood, Black Test Scores, and Affirmative Action" (VIDIO), December 11, 2012).

In America there is a government safety net with multiple welfare benefits such that one can survive safely without education and a job, whereas in Korea, one is ill prepared to survive without education and a job. Education in Korea is a lifeboat that can't be taken lightly. At the request of the US Congress, I submitted a nationwide survey study: *National Survey of Food Stamp and Food Distribution Program Recipients; A Summary of Findings on Income Sources and Amounts and Incidence of Multiple Benefits*, December 31 1974

(Washington, DC: US Government Printing Office, 1974). At the time, Congress was worried about stories concerning "welfare queens" milking the government; my mission was a fact-finding report. Some welfare recipients received up to eight multiple benefits that would beat working full time for some, contributing to more US long-term unemployment numbers. A recent study by Michael Tanner, *"The American Welfare State, How We Spend nearly $1 Trillion a Year---and Fail"*, Policy Analysis, CATO Institute, 2011.4.11, more clearly shows the scorcard of President Johnson's "Great Society" program.

HISTORY OF THE KOREAN CIVIL SERVICE EXAMINATIONS

The Goryeo (918–1392) and Joseon (1392–1910) Dynasties each lasted about five hundred years. Their citizens adopted the teachings of Confucius and Mencius as the mainstay of their ethical and educational standards far more fervently than the Chinese and Japanese did. All civil service positions in Korea require passing a rigid entry examination in reading and writing about the Chinese classics, ethics, and history, including poetry and essays. Upper-class boys start learning these subjects at age three and continue until they pass the exams in their late teens. Because of the years needed to master the Chinese classics, only upper-class boys can even attempt to take the tough civil service examinations.

Girls were excluded from schools and the public services until the nineteenth century. Today, Korea has a woman president and women cabinet officers, CEOs, university presidents, professional golfers, and even boxers.

The Korean civil service examinations began in 788 in the Silla Dynasty (57 BC–935 AD), following China's example, gained importance in the Goryeo Dynasty, and were the centerpiece of education in the Joseon Dynasty. Those who passed the advanced literary examinations came to monopolize the high positions of the state. Other less prestigious civil service examinations are military, medicine, geography, astronomy, Chinese classics, Japanese (language), and Mongolian (language).

Civil service examinations originated in 587 in China, but the Mongol's Yuan Dynasty (1271–1368) was not much interested in literary education and discontinued them. One story has it that a subjugated Chinese scholar told the khan (Mongol emperor) that you can conquer the world on horseback, but you can't rule it on horseback.

The Mongols moved the capital to China and hired a large number of educated Chinese civil servants. The Chinese Ming Dynasty chased out the Mongols and reinstated the civil service examinations system. The following Manchu Qing Dynasty (1644—1911), also a Mongol tribe, was assimilated into Chinese culture and continued the examinations.

Historically, most empires—Egypt, Alexander's Greece, Rome, Spain, Napoleon's France, Great Britain, Russia, Japan—eventually retreated to where they came from, but China's territorial expansion was an exception. The less-educated minority Mongolian Dynasties (Yuan and Qing) were assimilated into the more-educated majority Chinese.

Over time, the East Asian nations—China, Korea, and Japan—placed too much emphasis on classic Chinese literature, ignoring science and technology education. Since the sixteenth century the rulers of the East Asian nations often suppressed the teaching and development of technology for fear that new ideas and inventions would promote rebellion against the government; they also prohibited any contact with other nations. These three nations were then called the Hermit Kingdoms. Of the three hermits, Korea was the most isolated and backward.

One outstanding work was the invention of the Korean alphabet, now replacing the difficult Chinese characters. In 1446 King Saejong, the fourth king of the Joseon Dynasty, commissioned scholars of the Royal Academy to create a unique, simple phonetic alphabet called "Hangul"—which literally means "Korean writings"—for commoners and women who couldn't afford the time to learn to write Chinese.

This helped make the majority of people literate and transformed Korea into one of the world's most literate nations. It is rumored that King Saejong was looking over his garden through a framed window, and it dawned on him that the simple Korean window frame configuration would be familiar to everyone, and adopted this configuration as the model for the Korean alphabet.

EDUCATION FERVOR AND ACHIEVEMENT: EXAMPLES

The following Korean students—who had no money, no friends, little English, and no American school curriculum background—achieved, through a sheer fervor for learning, their educational goals at top US colleges.

These are not isolated cases; there are many more who studied in Korea or abroad and achieved their educational goals as well. These examples show that with a fervor for learning, anyone in the world—living in low-income areas of the United States or in a country wrecked by civil war, such as Korea was—regardless of background and financial status, can achieve his or her education and income goals.

This cause-and-effect equation applies to nations as well. There are no statistics that show a highly educated nation that is poor, or a poorly educated nation that is rich, unless it sits on gold or black gold. Education not only creates income, but it also infuses confidence into individuals, ethnic groups, and nations.

Recent evidence shows that governments' welfare programs, namely, their "social safety net" as advertised by vote-hungry politicians, are becoming undependable and unsafe as recession worsens; at the same time, the increasing financial outlay is bankrupting governments.

The most reliable safety net, therefore, is a safety net called education, which usually lasts a lifetime.

DR. JAE-PIL SEO

Seo was a doctor, a journalist, a noted champion of Korea's independence from Japan, the first Korean to become a naturalized US citizen (1890), and the founder of the first Korean newspaper in the Korean alphabet, the *Independent News.*

Seo was born to a poor noble family. At the age of eighteen, he passed the civil service exams, the youngest ever to do so, and became a junior officer in 1882. The following year he was sent to Japan to enroll at the forerunner of Keio University and the Toyama Army Academy. In July 1884 he returned to public service.

Seo advised the king that the Korean armed forces were obsolete and needed fundamental reform if they were not to fall victim to the imperialist powers. He was then appointed chief of the military training unit. In December 1884 Seo was involved in the Kapsin Coup led by Kim Ok-Gyun and served as his vice minister of defense. The coup was defeated in three days, as China intervened by sending troops.

Under the then "guilty by kinship" law, his parents, brothers, and sisters were executed, and his first wife, Lady Kim, was sold into slavery. She committed suicide rather than serve the term.

Many of the 1884 revolutionaries, including Seo, fled to Japan, and from Japan Seo moved to the United States. Seo considered Japan only a conduit for Western advanced knowledge, and he wanted to learn from the source.

Arriving in California in 1885, he spoke no English, had no friends or money, and faced racial discrimination. He worked at all sorts of odd jobs just to survive. Sometimes he did not get paid for his labor, but he had no legal recourse, as American citizens would have.

In 1886 Seo moved to Morrisontown, Pennsylvania, and attended the Harry Hillman Academy, thanks to the help of an American. He began to use the name "Philip Jaisohn" at that time. In 1890 he became the first Korean American to acquire US citizenship. He studied medicine at George Washington University and in 1892 was the first Korean to receive an American medical degree. In those days Asians were not granted citizenship and, like Jews, couldn't enter medical school, so Seo was an amazing exception.

In 1894 Seo married Muriel Armstrong, a niece of the former US President James Buchanan. Many opposed the marriage from concern that the union would not work in American society. But Seo's educational background and personal character must have saved the marriage, which lasted a lifetime. He and his wife had two daughters.

Seo wanted to stay at the medical school as an instructor, but when some students refused to attend his classes because he was Asian, he left the job.

In 1895 those involved in the Kapsin Coup were pardoned, enabling Jaisohn to return to Korea. The government wanted to appoint him foreign secretary, but he refused to take the position. He wanted to educate the common people about politics by publishing a newspaper, the *Independent News*. He was the first person to print a newspaper entirely in the Korean alphabet without any Chinese characters as he wanted to extend his readership to the lower classes and women. He was active in journalistic and political activities, and delivered regular lectures on modern politics and the principles of democracy. In 1897 Seo helped to construct the still standing Independence Gate in Seoul.

Seo was quite critical of corruption and misconduct of government officials, and so earned the displeasure of powerful people. The government in 1898 accused the Independent Club Seo organized of seeking to overthrow the monarchy so as to establish a republic. Following the arrest in late 1898 of seventeen of their leaders, including Rhee, Syngman (first president of the Korean Republic, 1948–1960), the organization was disbanded. Seo was forced to flee to the United States. His US citizenship might have saved his life.

Seo returned to practicing medicine and became a successful businessman in Philadelphia. He was also involved in medical research and published a number of articles in medical journals. During the Japanese colonial occupation beginning in 1910, Seo collaborated with Korean exiles to advance the cause of Korean independence by organizing, among other initiatives, the League of Friends of Korea in 1920.

Seo returned to Korea after the US liberation of Korea in 1945. He was invited by the US military to be an advisor in 1947. He felt uneasy about the country's gradual slide toward President Rhee's dictatorship. The chaotic conditions in Korea, combined with his advanced age, made it difficult for him to achieve much. Seo returned to the United States, where he died in 1951. He never saw the peaceful Korea he fought so hard for. The Korean government erected a bronze statue at the Korean embassy grounds in Washington, DC, in his memory.

DR. SYNGMAN RHEE

Rhee is another Korean student schooled in multiple languages and multiple cultures. He was born into a noble family of modest means. His early education was primarily in classic Chinese literature. He took the civil service examinations multiple times but always failed. Rhee enrolled in Paejae School, a missionary school, where he learned English and began a school newspaper. He joined the Independent Club, a political reform movement, in 1896. In the aftermath of a protest against Japanese dominance over Korea, Rhee was charged with sedition on January 9, 1899. He unsuccessfully attempted to escape imprisonment and was captured, tortured, and sentenced to life in prison.

Following the Russo-Japanese War, politics shifted in Korea, and Rhee was released from prison in 1904.

The Japanese forcefully used Korea as their military base during that war. At the behest of government officials, Rhee traveled to the United States to a peace conference to end the war. He arrived in Washington in December of that year, met with Secretary of State John Hay and President Roosevelt at peace conference talks in Portsmouth. He attempted to convince the United States to recognize the Korean kingdom as an independent nation. That failed, and Korea became a protectorate of Japan in 1905, and then a Japanese colony from 1910 to 1945.

Rhee remained in America for his education. By working odd jobs, he earned a BA from George Washington University in 1907, an MA from Harvard University in 1910, and a PhD from Princeton University the same year. His studies included politics, history, international relations, Christian theology, and law.

Rhee returned to Korea in late 1910 to become the chief secretary of the YMCA in Seoul. Fifteen months later, after Japan started to crack down on the Christian community in the nation, Rhee returned to the United States.

In 1919 all of the major pro-independent factions formed the Provisional Government of the Republic of Korea in Shanghai. Rhee was elected president, a post he held for six years. In 1925 he was removed from office for misusing his authority.

Rhee then lived in exile in Hawaii, New York, and Washington, where he worked in the Korean Independence Movement center. His Vienna-born wife, Franziska Donner, worked as his secretary, particularly in preparing the book *Japan Inside and Out* (1940).

After the defeat of Japan in World War II, Rhee was flown to Tokyo aboard a US military aircraft. Following a secret meeting with General Douglas MacArthur, Rhee was flown to Seoul in mid-October 1945 aboard MacArthur's personal airplane, *The Bataan.* Rhee was appointed head of the provisional Korean government that same year. He was then elected the first president of South Korea, defeating Kim Gu by a margin of 82 percent, on August 15, 1948.

Rhee governed his nation through the Korean War with help from the United States and fifteen other nations. After the war Rhee was easily reelected for three consecutive terms. In 1960 the 84-year-old Rhee won a fourth term with 90 percent of the vote; however, he was forced to resign on April 26, 1960, after a student-led demonstration about vote rigging that involved his protégé, Vice President Lee Gibung. The CIA flew Rhee and his wife to Honolulu. Rhee died of a stroke that July. A week later his body was returned to Seoul and buried in the National Cemetery. Mrs. Rhee went back to Austria for a while, but then returned to Korea, where she spent the rest of her life. She is buried by her husband.

Both President and Mrs. Rhee dedicated their lives to making Korea an independent nation. Rhee was not the most democratic president, to say the least, but he held the country in one piece for more than a decade despite chaotic political infighting and the Korean War. Unlike some succeeding Korean presidential families, the couple led a simple private life while in and after leaving office. It is rumored that First Lady Rhee was seen mending their socks during her spare time.

Both Seo and Rhee were forced into exile and secured the best education they could under the most difficult of circumstances, laying the foundation of modern Korea. Both of them became Korean education models for following generations of aspiring youngsters, as in the following examples.

MY FAMILY AND MY RELATIVES

Korean youth who stayed home, such as my father (born 1884), learned the Chinese classics first and then English, Japanese, math, and science. In the absence of our own textbooks, Koreans had to learn foreign languages to read English, Chinese, and Japanese books. When my father was studying, these books had to be imported. As Korea had no post office or banking system, I do not know how he obtained his books from overseas, including:

An Introduction to the "Arithmetical Analysis" by S. A. Felter

Elementary Algebra by C. Smith, translated by K. Nagasawa

New National Third Reader by N. H. Toda

New Language Lessons by William Swinton

Swinton's New First Reader by William Swinton

The Old Testament in two volumes, printed in Chinese on rice paper, Shanghai, late Qing period. (The original Korean Bible was translated from the Chinese version.)

My father also bought English lesson books with Chinese translations on rice paper from China. He studied geometry, which he needed for his job as a surveyor.

In 1902 he decided to go to America, the world's best source of advanced knowledge, and paid a hundred-dollar security deposit—one year's wage in Korea. He first arrived in Hawaii and then went to San Francisco; he was there during the famous earthquake. He returned home and served the last Korean king as a land surveyor.

The final years of the Joseon Dynasty were tumultuous ones. First there were the threats of Japan, China, and Russia vying for control over Korea, resulting in the Sino-Japanese War (1894–1895) and the Russo-Japanese War (1904–1905). The external threats turned into political infighting within the royal family and among various political factions. Under such external and internal chaos, Japan had an easy time of taking over Korea.

In fact, the Korean Royal Army had Japanese training instructors, which enabled Japanese Yakuza (unemployed ex-samurai) assassins to break into the Korean royal palace early in the morning and murder and set on fire the Korean queen, who opposed Japan's presence in Korea. The court in Japan freed all the assassins and promoted them to high government positions. This ended five hundred years of the Joseon Dynasty, and began thirty-five years of Japanese colonial control.

Around this turbulent period, Hawaiian sugar plantations needed farm workers and so set up a recruiting office in the port town of Busan, Korea. Many

Korean men applied for a job, seeking a better life in this unknown land. Later, some churches sponsored matchmaking for the plantation workers. The match-makers in Busan exchanged photos and biographies of interested parties. There was at least one incident in which a man cheated the bridal candidate by using another man's photo and biography and was rejected by his arriving bride at the Hawaiian port. A Korean pastor and his wife in the reception crowd offered to care for the dumbfounded and tearful girl until she settled the situation. In the meantime, the girl helped the pastor's household, looking after the children and doing the shopping.

One day, while shopping for groceries, she took a mis-step on the stairs, but a man behind her caught her before she and the groceries fell. That is how their romance began, and she eventually married this Korean man who had come to Hawaii for plantation labor but later became a foreman at a mining company.

As they started a family, he decided to change from the dangerous mining work to a safer occupation, and started a laundry on a military base. This soon became a chain, and the couple sent their six children to the best schools they could afford in the United States. They sent one of their daughters to Stanford University Medical School. She then married a Korean student studying at Harvard Medical School.

His parents had been killed when he was still in high school by North Korean soldiers when they occupied Seoul in 1950. His father was killed because he was a professor at Seoul University Medical School, and his mother was killed because she was a member of a women's civic group. Yet with help from a US Eighth Army chaplain, he went to a US college on a scholarship and then to Harvard. Dr. Andrew Kang and Dr. Ellen Kang served as professor of medicine at US universities, and their three daughters became doctor. All of them became exemplary US citizens thanks to their education and contributed greatly to the health of many Americans and people around the world.

4

My Education under the Japanese, Korean, and US Systems

I have been schooled in three different cultures and languages: elementary education in Japanese, secondary and college education in Korean, and a graduate program in English. I earned my BS in chemistry/ biochemistry in Korea and my PhD in economics/agricultural economics at the University of Minnesota.

My early schooling occurred during two wars: the Second World War (1939–1945), during which I was in the fourth to seventh grades, and the Korean War (1950–1953), which started when I was in twelfth grade. The wars interrupted about four years of classroom work but gave me a valuable lesson on survival in war and peace.

ELEMENTARY EDUCATION

I enrolled at the Su-Chang Elementary School in Daegu, Korea, when I was six-and-a-half-years old in 1938.

One of my classmates was the son of the founder of Samsung, who lived in my neighborhood. Lee Byung-Chul, the founder, operated a small noodle mill in town and set a good example of how fast one can become wealthy by producing products the country needed and then expanding to what the world needed, starting with noodles, flour, and sugar and expanding to textiles, construction, department stores, hospitals, radio and TV, financial services, shipbuilding, and IT. Samsung is still controlled by his family members. Along the way, Samsung employed many science, technology, and business majors in Korea and overseas, generating more employment and income for Korea and the world.

During the Japanese colonial period when I was going to school, education was not compulsory or free; fewer than 40 percent of student-age children received elementary education. In 1948, under the US military administration, the attendance rate jumped to 75 percent. Now everyone receives free preschool, elementary (first through sixth grade), and middle school (seventh through ninth grade) education in Korea.

The profile of my elementary school is as follows:

Students: 1,680

Classroom size: 70 students in each class

Classes in each grade: 4 (2 for girls and 2 for boys)

Grades: 6

Teachers: 24, who also performed all administrative and support duties

PRINCIPAL: JAPANESE

There was also a janitor who did only school maintenance and repairs. Students did all the cleaning: classrooms, windows, grounds, and toilets. Another notable feature of the Japanese school was administrative and support duties were done by the principal and 24 teachers.

The class started at eight in the morning. All students arrived at 7:30 to mop the room, scrub the windows, and clean the blackboard. All cleaning had to pass a white-glove inspection by the head of the class. We then headed out to the school grounds and lined up in military formation by class and grade, and the principal led us in the ceremonial bowing to the emperor in Tokyo. Then all students marched back to the classrooms in military precision and waited, with their eyes and mouths closed, for the teacher to enter the room. As the teacher opened the door, the head of class yelled, "Attention!" We all stood up, bowed to the teacher, and sat down. Students had to pay close attention to the teacher for forty-five minutes no yawing, chatting, or making funny faces.

Any kind of misbehavior was corrected with a long bamboo stick. For repeat offenders, the teacher would order the student to bring his or her parents to school for a conference, and would ask the parents to properly discipline the child at home, warning them that there would not be another chance. Once dismissed for misbehavior, no other public school would accept the student. I have seen teachers beat a student until the bamboo stick broke, though I was never subjected to such physical punishment myself. When students broke or damaged school property, the parents had to pay for it.

Japanese and Korean teachers were generally kind and thoughtful. The golden rule was not breaking the school rules or upsetting the teacher. However, students were subjected to punishment by association. If a member of the group did not line up straight in formation, we all had to regroup until we got it right like boot camp.

Mandatory subjects were ethics, Japanese, arithmetic (which included using an abacus), Japanese history, geography, science, painting (including drawing and penmanship), music, physical education, and—for girls—homemaking. There were no electives. All students received the same mandatory subjects, and extra activities such as painting, music, and sports were allowed on an individual basis after regular school hours.

Each student had an assigned desk in the seventy-student classroom, small students in the front so that the teacher could see better what each one was doing and who was missing. Children were responsible for maintaining and cleaning their own desks. Although it was a coed school, to avoid problems, the classrooms were not coed.

Usually one teacher taught the majority of the subjects for each class—except certain skills such as painting, music, and using the abacus—so that the teacher and students would know each other better

On December 8, 1941, when I was in fourth grade, the school gathered all teachers and students into the auditorium and the Japanese principal announced that Japan had declared war against America, England, and other allies. We children had no idea what to expect of the war, of course. The declaration of war sounded like an exciting big game among the nations. When I told my father, he only said, "This is a match between a kid and a grownup—no contest!" His prediction was correct.

As the stream of victorious news came through for the first few months—including the taking of Hong Kong, Singapore, and Manila—all students were asked to march in the streets in formation with the Japanese flag waving, singing Japanese marching songs. The victory songs and dances stopped as the US Navy and Army took back what the United States lost in the Pacific, such as the Philippines and Guam.

Korean schoolchildren were then turned into child laborers, given strenuous jobs like removing rocks from military cave construction sites from six in the morning onward. I had to get up in the dark around five to get to the mountain site. We had no sneakers or sturdy shoes, and all children had to wear straw shoes to protect their feet from the sharp-edged dynamited rocks.

We worked hard in total silence to avoid harsh punishment. No sick students were allowed to skip the hard labor without a doctor's statement, and in those days we had only a few doctors in town. Once I had a bad eye infection for a week and couldn't see daylight, but that was not a good enough reason to stay home. Children were served a baseball-size rice ball sprinkled with a little salt and one apple. The Japanese government broke all the child labor rules!

Sometimes the children working at the airfield cleaning the Japanese Kamikaze Zero fighter planes saw the young pilots practicing takeoffs—perhaps because no landing practice was necessary for their mission.

I saw *The Bridge on the River Kwai* when I was a student at the University of Minnesota, and the war prisoner's life in the movie reminded me of my grade school life during World War II. The only difference between the British prisoners in the movie and me was I was in my own home and eating rationed home meals. Not that the home meals were any better than those of the British prisoners. We ate all sorts of wild edible mountain vegetables and plants, milling wastes (normally livestock feed) to supplement scarce grains, salted or dried fish, and vegetables.

One thing about wartime Japanese society was that everyone, high and low, suffered fairly equally. Admiral Yamamoto, the Japanese naval chief shot down by a group of US fighters on his way to inspect naval bases in the South Pacific islands, made a last visit to his family before he went to the Pacific command. His family had no last dinner for him; they bought bowls of noodle soup from a street vendor. Yamamoto predicted to his fellow officers when the war started that if Japan couldn't conclude the war by victory or a peace settlement within a year and a half, they would lose. He had served as a naval attaché in Washington and had attended Harvard University, and thus knew more about US affairs than the war hawks in the Japanese Army.

Throughout my elementary school years, the 1,680 students obeyed the harsh, Spartan, boot camp discipline in silence. We had no time or extra energy for bullying other students or engaging in mischief, as happens in some Korean primary and secondary schools today.

Perhaps the Spartan-type elementary education is the lowest cost and most effective disciplinary method to minimize school bullying. This low-cost education climate also produced one enviable result: I became a survivor at home in Korea and abroad in America. My classmates included general, Korean UN representative, the Samsung Group family, Korean government minister, CEO of Japanese firm, and many other fine individuals. Nations with limited financial resources and teaching and support staff can emulate this Japanese wartime education model, modified by their own cultural standards.

Lately, Korean elementary and high school education systems have started emulating the US model of free education from preschool to ninth grade. Unlike the American school lunch program where free, reduced price, and paid lunch is based on family income and household size, the Korean program is free to all so that low-income children are not embarrassed in front of their classmates. But the Korean program has a fatal defect in that an all-free-lunch approach can break the budget, as has already happened in many Korean school districts.

I have participated in the design of the US school lunch and Food Stamp Program and have published a paper that is designed to reduce US school lunch costs by about 10 percent (J. C. Chai, "School Food Procurement: Procurement Models and Guides," *School Food Service Research Review*, Vol. 3, November 1, 1979).

With socialized education, schools tend to treat all children equally regardless of differences in physical condition, mental brightness, family early childhood training, and personal preferences.

The public school system forces children who dislike school to stay there, where they feel like they are being kept in a cage. With compulsory education, these children feel hemmed in and buck the system by skipping classes, misbehaving, and disturbing everyone else. This is happening in the United States and elsewhere. The misbehaving students may be only a few, but they can easily upset an entire class or school, and the resulting social costs are huge.

Society does not need only lawyers and doctors. It needs different talents in various professions. Some of these "wild" students today could make excellent future boxers, Olympians, special forces members, entertainers, or even philosophers. The government, instead of mixing every child together in the same classroom, should support private or government-run special professional/vocational/skill schools for otherwise talented children in line with their natural talents.

SECONDARY EDUCATION

I finished six years of elementary school in February 1945, having spent less time on study and more time doing slave labor. I began my six-year secondary education at Daegu Commercial School, where about half of the students were Japanese. The Japanese at the time had two types of secondary education systems: the general high school and the vocational high school. They placed great emphasis on vocational education to catch up with the West in the agricultural, commercial, and technical industries.

All admissions were based on academic tests and physical examinations, including vision tests. Japanese students were selected first at a lower cutoff score; then Korean students were accepted with a higher cutoff. This unfair practice forced Korean students to work harder than their Japanese classmates just to stay even.

The majority of teachers were Japanese, and an army officer was assigned for the military training class. Students spent much of regular study time doing forced labor or in military training, preparing for an American landing.

Japanese radio stations and newspapers never gave a true picture of the war. When the United States dropped atomic bombs on Hiroshima and Nagasaki in August, just before the Japanese unconditional surrender, I remember the Japanese news media mentioned only that the United States had dropped "parachute bombs" and the cities suffered "minor damage." We all assumed the bombs were delivered by parachute; we didn't picture the mushroom or parachute shape of the explosions. By then the Japanese military and scientists must have known about the destructive power of the US atomic bomb, but the Japanese government never used the word "atomic" in order to hide the awful destructive facts from the public.

On August 15, 1945, I heard the news of the Japanese surrender while under a bridge where a group of students slept overnight on our way home from working all day at a remote country farm. Koreans celebrated the news with joy, but most Japanese did not say a word. They were just exhausted. I am sure they were glad that the unspeakable misery had come to an end.

The Japanese are trained to obey their parents at home, teachers at school, and superiors in the office, and so they obeyed the victorious American soldiers. I watched Japanese soldiers obediently sweeping the US Army compound that used to be theirs. They are, perhaps, the most orderly and obedient individuals on earth. However, there were a few exceptions.

On August 14 a group of hotheaded, low-ranking Japanese officers risked their lives trying to inter-cept the imperial surrender tape being delivered to the Tokyo radio station; upon failing to intercept it, some committed suicide. The Japanese Air Force gen-eral who initiated the Kamikaze attack flew his last solo mission upon hearing the surrender and was the last Kamikaze pilot. For some Japanese, honor comes before all else, even death. The Japanese call it "Bushido," the way of the samurai (knight).

All Japanese residents had to leave formerly occu-pied Korea on short notice no easy feat when some had been there for thirty years. I saw no disorderly conduct from the Japanese and no vengeance against them for their unspeakable mistreatment of Koreans. My sixth-grade Japanese teacher gave his home to one of my classmates. He and his wife were glad that the war was finally over but felt sad to leave Korea and the students he taught. In China there were some incidents of revenge, but some Chinese families also adopted and raised orphaned Japanese children. War always displays the good and bad sides of the human race.

The Japanese, however, left Korea in a mess: treeless mountains, waterless rivers, and broken towns. The Japanese—using Korean laborers, including school children—had cut down all the trees for fuel and resin for military and civilian uses. Lacking gas and oil resources, they used charcoal to run the buses and trucks. The charcoal bus engines often couldn't climb the hills, at which point all the passengers would get out and push the bus up the hills. Even the leaves under the trees were raked clean for fuel. The rain would cause flooding, followed by a waterless river on dry days. As a result, many plant species and wild animals, including Korean tigers, became extinct.

The Japanese also demolished several rows of homes and shops along both sides of city streets to prevent fire from spreading from American bombs, leaving all major Korean cities looking bombed out even without air raids. I saw a B-29 flying high over the Korean sky, leaving a long white streak behind, but it never dropped a bomb on Korea. The Japanese did all the destruction of Korean towns and the countryside.

Human resources also were in a pitiful state. Koreans were not quite prepared to fill the gaps the Japanese had left. When Japan colonized Korea in 1910, Koreans were in cabinet posts while the Japanese held advisory positions; then, in a very short time, the Japanese replaced even the mid- and low-ranking posts, such as school principals, railroad stationmasters, and teachers.

The US military administration governed South Korea from 1945 to 1948 and introduced an American education system. It did a superb job in introducing and vitalizing Korean education programs under awful conditions. Not only did Korea not have enough qualified teachers, but there also were no Korean textbooks other than what the Japanese had left.

All Korean students had to start learning the basic Korean alphabet and Korean language in 1945 because the Japanese had forbidden speaking Korean at school. Up through twelfth grade, half of my study time was spent learning Korean, English, and the Chinese classics.

In the absence of Korean textbooks, I relied on Japanese texts all through college. Schools didn't have libraries so I used the city library, which carried mostly outdated Japanese books. I went to bookstores just to browse through new Japanese books. Sometimes I would memorize important sections of a book and then record it at home.

My secondary school curriculum included ethics, Korean, English, mathematics, German (or French or Chinese), geography, physics, chemistry, business (economics and accounting), and physical education. I took sports as an elective.

The vocational secondary schools included subjects on their special fields, such as agriculture or industry. All secondary students could change their major after graduation and apply for a college or university of their choice.

During my secondary school years my interest was in chemistry. I set up a chemistry lab in my house. I made soap using shark oil, the cheapest oil available in those days, but it was too soft and smelled awful. Soy sauces are made in two ways, by fermentation or chemically. The fermentation takes a few months and the chemical process takes a few hours. The instant soy sauces use soy meals (plant protein) and hydrochloric acid, neutralized with soda to produce salt and amino acids in the soy sauces. Just for kicks, I tried hair (animal protein) instead of soy meal (vegetable protein). It had, to my surprise, a somewhat similar flavor as real soy sauces. I did all sorts of crazy things and became known in my hometown as the "crazy boy chemist."

However, my crazy hobby led to real danger when the Korean War started during my senior year. Early one morning I was picked up by the South Korean Military Secret Agency (nicknamed the "white skull" troop for their indiscriminate killings) for interrogation. They thought North Korean communists might use me for making chemical weapons or other lethal devices when they took over the town, so the Secret Agency wanted to eliminate me.

The interrogator placed a pencil between my fingers and tried to get me to write a pain-induced confession. A few moments later my family, through a govern-ment connection, arrived and pulled me out of danger just in time. Fortunately, my hometown was spared from invasion. The North Korean troops reached the city limits and started shelling our town. Then the re-grouped American and South Korean forces pushed them back north.

The Korean War was even more savage and devas-tating economically and emotionally for Korea than the Second World War. It was primarily the result of the mistaken division of Korea by the victorious

Allies. The Soviet Union wanted a portion of Japan for its part in the war. The mistake was that the United States considered Korea a part of the Japanese empire and felt the Koreans were "too uneducated" (brainwashed by the Japanese since 1900) to manage their own affairs.

Western political leaders of the time forgot that most empires had been built by uneducated but gutsy leaders: the Mongols' Genghis Kahn, the first emperor of the Ming dynasty, and the first emperor of the Qing dynasty had never been to school, but they were phenomenal conquerors, builders, and leaders of great empires. On the other hand, their succeeding and well-educated emperors lost the great empires that their "uneducated" forefathers had built.

The people who would become the Koreans migrated from Mongolia over five thousand years ago and settled in Korea. Some migrated to Japan and established a settlement near the northern Kyushu region, from which the early Japanese kingdom emerged. The successive Korean dynasties survived Mongol, Manchu, Chinese, and frequent Japanese military and pirate invasions.

The Allies, understandably, knew very little about the history and people of Korea. The State Department did not even have a decent map of Korea; indeed, one of its staff found a Korean map in a *National Geographic* magazine and thought the 38th parallel line looked close to the middle of the Korean peninsula. Thus began the three-year military administration of divided Korea, overseen by the Soviet Union for the North and the United States for the South.

After the Allies' military administration ended, the Soviet Union backed the Stalinist regime of Kim Il-Sung (former Soviet Union Army captain) and equipped North Korea with combat aircraft, tanks, and artillery. The United States backed the administration of President Rhee, but supplied only light military equipment, a small amount of field artillery, with no tanks or combat aircraft. The United States wanted to discourage President Rhee from his expressed desire of unifying the country through military force.

The factors that encouraged Kim to attack South Korea were, first, US Secretary of State Acheson's plan that Korea not be included in the strategic Asian Defense Perimeter, and second, Stalin giving Kim permission to invade South Korea, under the condition that Mao Zedong would send reinforcements if needed.

The greatly unbalanced military power between North and South Korea—along with Stalin's and Mao's military support as opposed to the American "forget

Korea" policy (some Americans call the Korean War "the Forgotten War")—invited Kim to attack the South on June 25, 1950. He took the capital city, Seoul, on June 28, and the retreating South Korean Army blew up the Han River Bridge to hinder North Korea's advance. This unfortunately exposed the remaining Seoul citizens to the whims of civil war. Many innocent citizens were summarily executed by North Korean soldiers.

The United States then provided 88 percent of the 341,000 international soldiers, with fifteen other UN countries offering assistance. Suffering severe casualties within the first two months, the defenders were pushed back to a small area in the south of Korea known as the Busan perimeter, which included my town, Daegu. A rapid UN counteroffensive then drove the North Koreans back past the 38th parallel and almost to the Yalu River (bordering China), when China entered the war and forced the Allies to retreat behind the 38th parallel. The fighting ended on July 27, 1953, when the armistice agreement was signed.

The total force fighting for South Korea at the moment of cease-fire was 932,911 from seventeen nations: Republic of Korea, United States, United Kingdom, Philippines, Thailand, Canada, Turkey, Australia, New Zealand, Ethiopia, Greece, France, Colombia, Belgium, South Africa, Netherlands, and Luxembourg.

The total strength of the opposing side was 1,642,600 troops from North Korea, China, and the Soviet Union. The casualty estimates on both sides are as follows:

1. South Korea: 137,899 military deaths, 377,599 civilian deaths, 229,625 civilian wounded, 387,744 abducted/missing

2. United States: 33,686 battle deaths, 8,176 missing in action

3. China: 400,000 battle deaths, 486,000 wounded

4. North Korea: 215,000 battle deaths, 303,000 wounded

As mentioned earlier, the Korean War is often called the Forgotten War. We all wish it never took place. This was the first global war, involving soldiers from all continents except Antarctica, and 2.6 million soldiers from twenty nations killing each other in a very small area, roughly the size of Idaho.

MY THREE HEROES OF THE KOREAN WAR

Of the 2.6 million soldiers engaged in the war, I admire three Americans the most. My admiration is not for their bravery or their military accomplishments, but for their just being fine soldiers. They did their duty the best they could and sacrificed for a country they knew little about. All others from the seventeen nations did the same, deserving heartfelt appreciation from all South Koreans, but these three are special to me.

First is General Walton Walker, the US Eighth Army commander, who died on December 23, 1950, when his jeep collided with a civilian truck while he was directing the battle near Seoul. (The Korean government has named the spot Walker Hill in his memory.) I admire General Walker because he stayed with his soldiers during the heat of battle and risked his life for Korea. As a commanding officer, he could have stayed behind, avoiding the dangers of the front line. He does not have a war record like General MacArthur, but he stayed and died with his men. During World War II General MacArthur left the Philippines for the safety of Australia, leaving his fighters with the famous "I shall return" speech. Indeed, he did return to the old battlefield, but many of his soldiers had already died a miserable death during the Bataan Death March, and the survivors ended up in awful Japanese prison camps. None of them had the chance to welcome their returning hero wading onto the shore of the Philippines.

Second is General William F. Dean, the US Twenty-Fourth Division commander who was given command of all US forces—with only 15,965 men and

4,773 vehicles to hold the overwhelming forces of North Korea at bay. On July 20, 1950, General Dean ordered the retreat of the his division headquarters in Daejon to the south, but he remained behind and assisted the US troops in evacuating the city until the last convoy was ready. He and his men fought through North Korean roadblocks and ambushes, and General Dean stopped his jeep to tend to several wounded soldiers in a wrecked truck in a ditch. While he was going after water for a wounded man, General Dean fell down a steep slope and was knocked unconscious. When he regained consciousness, he found he had a gashed head, a broken shoulder, and many bruises.

For thirty-six days General Dean wandered alone in the mountains trying to reach safety, going without food and medical treatment. The six-foot-one-inch-tall man was reduced to 130 pounds. On August 25 he was caught and made a prisoner of war. He remained defiant during interrogation, refusing to divulge any information and acting unafraid, sometimes laughing off threats. He was never actually tortured. He was given better treatment than most UN prisoners in North Korea, as he was regularly fed and rarely subjected to interrogations after his initial capture. His impeccable world-class solider-gentleman character must have impressed the enemy.

He was returned to UN forces at Panmunjom on September 4, 1953, and given a ticker-tape parade in New York City upon his return on September 26.

Third is General Francis T. Dodd, commanding officer of the Koje-do POW camp. One of the most humiliating events for the UN forces during the Korean War took place on May 7, 1952, when Camp Commandant General Dodd was taken prisoner in a camp uprising and put on trial for abuse of prisoners, a farce unequalled in all military history. The genesis of this farce was the Geneva Convention of 1949 on prisoners of war. It was designed primarily to protect prisoners and completely failed to provide protection for captor nations in dealing with organized armed resistance, as was the case at Koje-do POW camp. At the camp, a mini Korean War was going on among 170,000 Chinese and North Korean POWs, roughly divided by 70,000 who wanted repatriation and 100,000 who did not.

The prisoner uprising was well planned. North Korea sent in an army general disguised as a buck private to be captured and sent to the camp as a POW. He took command of organizing the camp's resistance and led the daily beating and murdering of anti-Communist prisoners. They crafted knives and other weapons from tin cans and oil drums.

After winning as many concessions as they thought they could obtain, the Communists finally released General Dodd. He was relieved of his command, reduced in rank to colonel, and forced to retire the next year. Four years after his death, in January 1977, General Dodd was posthumously restored to his previous rank. The former US Eighth Army commander General Van Fleet extolled, "No one, I repeat, no one could have done a better job."

To Koreans, the Korean War was a horribly destructive and sad experience, but in the process, we learned many valuable lessons and won a chance for a fresh start, helped by the United States. Korea up until the nineteenth century was known as the last Asian Hermit Kingdom, steeped in the Chinese classics, avoiding science and technology education and the outside world. The Korean War brought in the outside world.

A new seed of opportunity for education was planted through the USAID program, which rekindled Koreans' fervor for education. These US-trained faculty members are the ones who helped to build Seoul University into the Harvard of the Korean education system, the most prestigious university in Korea, and became the model for Korean education.

SCHOOLS DURING THE KOREAN WAR

All schools were closed, along with many government functions, during much of the three years of civil war. As in America's frontier days, every man was out for himself, and Korea was a dangerous place to be. North Korea took control of much of South Korea with such speed that the South Korean Army suffered high casualties. It needed replacement recruits quick. The army sent out trucks to load up as many boys from the street corners as they could without checking age or notifying the family; they sent them to a one-week training camp and then to the frontlines. Many of my classmates recruited in such a fashion did not come home. The North did the same thing to their occupied regions. The North Korean army killed anyone who held high positions, the wealthy, and suspected non-Communists. It drafted the remaining young people into its force. My brother was teaching high school chemistry in the North Korean occupied zone and was taken away with some of his fellow teachers. We still do not know what happened to him. The South Korean civilian death toll (377,599) far exceeds the military death toll (137,899). Being in the army was statistically safer than being a civilian during the Korean War.

Fortunately, I found a job working for an US Army unit when it was stationed in my hometown of Daegu; I became a member of the American unit as a Korean civilian employee and saw the war up close. As the US Army pushed the North Korean Army back, my supply unit followed the frontline and moved to Daejon, Suwon, and then to Seoul when American forces landed in Inchon and recovered the capital in late September. When my unit arrived in Seoul, the major streets were filled with destroyed North Korean tanks and trucks, and our unit settled into elementary school buildings behind the government capital building complex. I walked around the hills behind the complex and saw the half-buried bodies of North Korean soldiers scattered around.

On January 4, 1951, the American infantry was being pushed back from near the Manchurian border to Seoul, covered in yellow dust and looking tired, but they were very orderly and even in a joking mood. We all shared the same school buildings, with some settling in heatless hallways in their sleeping bags. The freezing cold Korean winter was much colder that year.

Then it was our unit's turn to retreat. We burned anything we couldn't carry, such as extra fuel that the enemy might use. While we retreated, broken vehicles were pushed to the roadsides and burned. In order to mitigate my motion sickness, I lay down on the narrow center of the army jeep. We stopped at a few places overnight and ended up in Daegu, where

I had the opportunity to visit my family. Fortunately, Daegu and Busan (the second- and third-largest cities in Korea) were untouched by the war.

The regrouped UN forces pushed the North Koreans and Chinese forces back to the area of the 38th parallel. My unit returned to Seoul and settled in the same school buildings. I had a rare opportunity to attend Bob Hope's show at a theater in Seoul. The GIs and I had the best and most memorable time of our lives. My unit moved north to Yijungbu and then moved northeast, closer to the frontline. When we found no large building to accommodate our company, we pitched our tents on the riverbed for the water supply—it was more sanitary and easier to guard than locations near the hill or village.

Around that time there were disagreements between President Truman, who wanted to end the war to avoid more casualties, and General MacArthur, who wanted to finish the job. On-again, off-again armistice negotiations continued for two years until July 1953.

I left the US military unit to receive my high school diploma, although I did not attend class my entire senior year from June 1950 to June 1951. All schools were being occupied by US and Korean military units, so the school pitched a tent on the empty riverbed to conduct its graduation ceremony. Only about 50 percent of my former classmates attended and received their diploma; the rest may be lost in action. We all were lucky to attend the ceremony, and no one complained about missed classes.

COLLEGE EDUCATION

I passed the required college entrance examinations in March 1952 (the Korean school year is normally March to March) for Kyungbook National University, College of Agriculture, and majored in agricultural chemistry (which included the study of biochemistry, food science, soil science, and microbiology).

All the college campuses were being occupied by the US and Korean military, so all lectures were held in temporary huts during the harsh Korean winter. The basic freshman subjects, such as principles of economics, had two hundred or more students in each class. There was no library for the more than ten thousand students at the university—a situation common to all schools in Korea at the time.

Recognizing our plight, the US Eighth Army offered to build a few rows of temporary one-story wooden buildings in the style of army barracks. I served as translator between the university and the US Army Corps of Engineers that did the construction work. The commander of the Corps of Engineers, a major, told me that General Maxwell Taylor, the commander of the US Eighth Army, would visit to look at the completed construction. I related the message to the university dean.

On a fine fall afternoon, around three o'clock, I saw a long line of military vehicles coming down to the campus, headed up by MP jeeps, then General Taylor's jeep, followed by the vehicles of the *Stars and Stripes* reporters.

General Taylor, a slim and fine-featured gentleman in combat uniform, with one hand grenade at each shoulder ready for surprise attacks, greeted us with a relaxed smile. I introduced my dean and faculty members and led him and his MP escorts around the new construction site. Everyone seemed very pleased and relaxed, except the major in charge of the construction.

Upon the general's departure, the major was hopping mad that the university had not had a flag-waving welcoming party for the general. In those years, the US Army commander lorded it over the Japanese emperor and the Korean president. When the US commander went places, the Korean government prompted people to line the streets, waving both the Stars and Stripes and the Korean flag. On such occasions, the government provided additional military and police protection for the visiting dignitary. However, this particular visit was unannounced, and the university couldn't cancel all its classes to cheer the general.

I related to my dean why the major was displeased. The dean's reply was that, according to Korean custom, we would have a big ceremony prior to the construction to repel any evil spirits, but no big ceremony after the uneventful completion. Perhaps the spirits want an advance payment of respect and nothing else later. I related this explanation to the major, but he couldn't quite digest it. After the major left the school, my dean decided to have one of the Mennonite missionaries in town act as an intermediary to explain things to the major. I thought of telling my dean to just let it go—the major would cool down sooner or later. But I was just a student, and it was not my place to decide school matters.

We went to visit Mr. Weaver, head of the Canadian Mennonite Aid Mission in Korea, at the Daegu Missionary Compound. Douglas Cozart answered the door to say that Mr. Weaver was out. He added, "I just arrived in Daegu from America last week to start a Bible correspondence school in Korea, and need a Korean language teacher and translator for my mission work." He offered me the job on the spot. I told him I was not Christian, but he said that was OK.

Because of the testy incident with the major, l got a job teaching Korean to an American missionary and helped him carry out his mission work in Korea. l also organized free English conversation classes once a week by inviting an American army signal company commander and a USAID official, Mr. Maybe. My class was always full and became very popular. l met Mr. Maybe again when l was working at the US Department of Agriculture (USDA) in Washington, and he became a longtime friend.

Mr. Cozart was a single man with a full-time maid. He asked me to move into his house so that l could work for him during the hours l wasn't attending school. He also bought me a bicycle so as to cut down on my commuting time between the office and the university. l was one busy student attending university classes, organizing and conducting English classes for my fellow students, and translating for my boss and his many visiting Americans.

One day l invited Mr. Cozart to my home. My father came to greet him in full formal Korean attire. He spoke English, for he had spent some years in Hawaii and San Francisco. My father mentioned to his American guest that the West and the East have exact opposite ethics on dress codes. ln the West, when a guest visits a home, the man takes off his hat and coat. ln the East, the host must be fully dressed with hat and coat on. I had never noticed this until my father mentioned it.

Mr. Cozart rented office space for the correspondence school in downtown Daegu, with about ten office staff mailing out Bible lesson materials and test sheets, and then returning the corrected tests to students. Our students included individuals, groups, churches, and even prisons—including the Chinese and North Korean POW camp in Geoje island, where the rioting POWs took General Dodd hostage.

The Cozart home became a Korean Union Station for a large number of American evangelists and aid organizations interested in spreading the gospel and donating necessities to needy Koreans. I enjoyed meeting and interpreting for these fine visitors, among whom were leaders of World Vision, Campus Crusade, and Youth for Christ. I worked for Mr. Cozart until the office moved to Seoul during my college senior year, when the devastated city was cleared and reconstructed enough to function as the nation's capital.

UNIVERSITY OF MINNESOTA

I graduated after four years of college—without any war interruptions this time. Korea was still in the "cottage industry" stage and had no industry that could hire college science graduates. With no prospects for a job, I decided to do my graduate work in the United States, but I had no one who could guide me through the admissions process and tell me about tuition, living costs, and other details. I visited Professor Snyder in Seoul, the head of the University of Minnesota–Seoul University USAID program, and started to apply as a self-funded student. I went through the necessary Korean government and US embassy English test and interview. I also needed an "affidavit of support," and Dr. Bob Pierce, the founder of World Vision, whom I translated for a few times while he was visiting Korea, gladly signed the paper. I told him I would manage my own financial affairs in the States, and I did. I was admitted to graduate school on conditional status because of my change from an undergraduate major in chemistry to graduate studies in economics—agricultural economics as my major and food technology as a minor.

The major obstruction to going to college in Korea or overseas is the high cost of tuition and school-related expenses. About 35 percent of American college students drop out because of financial reasons. For foreign students, the costs and problems of going to an American college far exceed that of American students because foreign students must pay out-of-state tuition at state institutions, have no government student loans, no bank loans, and no scholarships unless they obtain one at the time of admission. If I had known all these fine points, I would have never gone to the States to study. I came because I did not know. When I knew, it was too late to back-up and pack-up. I had to move forward and just do it!

I was the youngest of nine siblings, and by then my father had passed away and my mother was in her early sixties. My parents had land holdings, but real estate sales were slow at the time. I had been financially independent since twelfth grade through various jobs, but I didn't have enough savings to pay my tuition and living expenses in America, so my mother helped me. I needed a minimum of six hundred dollars (this was when a US postage stamp cost three cents) to take care of my expenses for a couple of quarters. I had a hundred-dollar bill and needed five hundred dollars more. I asked my former boss, Mr. Cozart, if he would exchange, at the official exchange rate, the five hundred I needed. To my surprise, he said my money is God's money and asked the black market exchange rate, which was three times the official rate. I said no thanks.

I thought Professor Snyder might need some pocket money in Korean currency while in Korea, and asked for foreign exchange. Again, to my surprise, he said yes. I had a few send-off parties by my friends in Daegu and was also invited by Mr. Koo, the founder of the LG Group, for a sumptuous dinner at his traditional Korean-style mansion in Seoul. Mr. Koo, a friend of my brother-in-law, is an industrial giant, who got his start making toothpaste.

Korea did not have an international airport and no airline at the time, so l went to a military airstrip called Yeido Airport, which was just a few tin barracks by the Han River, where the Korean congressional buildings now stand. Before getting on the Northwest Airline plane, l had to go through a customs inspection line. The Korean inspector found a hundred-dollar bill in my wallet and confiscated it, saying that Koreans were not allowed to carry foreign currency. l and my friend, an army colonel, argued the obviously illegal and illogical confiscation of money from a student going to study in America, where American currency is needed immediately upon landing in an American airport for transportation fare to the school. In the meantime, the plane took off. Apparently, Korean law stated that Korean citizens couldn't have foreign currency on Korean soil. l lost the argument and money, missed the scheduled departure, had to take the next flight one week later, and pay a 10 percent late tuition fee at the University of Minnesota a bad luck multiplier effect!

On the flight to Minnesota, l looked down at Korea: treeless mountains, waterless rivers, broken cities, and a nasty government a land of no hope! l said to myself, "I shall *not* return." I kept my silent promise for a while, but I returned to my old nest in the end.

My first stopover was Tokyo. At the baggage pickup I chanced upon Dr. Pierce, my financial sponsor, and told him I am on my way to the University of Minnesota. He suggested I spend one night at the Imperial Hotel, where he was staying, as his guest. I walked the city of Tokyo, including the back streets. Japan at the time was still not fully recovered from the awful incendiary bombing; many men still wore leftover Japanese army uniforms and worked in silence.

The plane stopped over at a small island off Alaska to refuel and then landed at the Seattle airport, where I had to transfer to another plane. I stopped by a restroom with a ten-cent sign on the door, and I did not have a penny. My pocket money had been confiscated by that Korean customs inspector, renewing my distaste for the Korean government.

The sky view of Minnesota contrasted dramatically with Korea: endless green fields dotted with numerous blue lakes. Before going to the university campus for my housing and registration, I had to cash Professor Snyder's personal check at his brother's Snyder Drug Store in downtown Minneapolis. I took a cab, cashed the five hundred dollars, ran back out to pay the cab, and had my first breakfast in America at the drugstore. I asked Mr. Willy Snyder to keep my two suitcases until I found housing that afternoon.

I went to the Minneapolis campus and paid my tuition, including the late fees, and took a school bus to the St. Paul campus, where the agricultural campus was located. By then, I was exhausted from stress, motion sickness, and jet lag. I needed some rest or else I would fall down. On the bus, I said to a student next to me that I had just come "off the boat" from Korea and needed a quiet place to take a brief rest. He said he was also a new student from Hawaii for a graduate program in agricultural economics. He offered to take me to the university hospital at the St. Paul campus, where his wife was a nurse. She might be able to find me an empty bed. I napped for a couple of hours, went to the housing office, and found a house where two Seoul University professors shared an attic room. I became the third roomer. The rent was twenty-five dollars a month without a kitchen.

Then I had to pick up my suitcases from Snyder Drug Store. My landlord was willing to drive me to the store. I told him the location was Snyder Drug Store, but he said that was a chain and he needed an address. I did not remember the address. Fortunately, I did remember the name of the store owner, so we stopped at the nearest Snyder Drug Store and asked for Willy Snyder.

The required credit load for graduate school was nine credits, but I took twelve credits for the first quarter: three economics courses and one microbiology course.

I did not know that winters were colder in Minnesota than in Korea. The attic room was very dry from the constantly blowing hot furnace air, and I started getting nosebleeds every morning. After taking a Thanksgiving visit without a coat to Mountain Lake, Minnesota, where my old Mennonite missionary friend lived, I got Hong Kong flu. I ended up at the university hospital in an isolation ward for over a week, missing all of my classes. My first quarter I received one F in macroeconomics, but I had the highest class test score of 90 in microbiology, and that saved me from being dismissed because I had to maintain a B average as a graduate student. My microbiology professor suggested that I transfer to the University of Oregon, where I would get the best PhD program in food science and technology. However, I had no funds to move to another state, and physically I was in no condition to move.

The spring quarter came and I moved from the three-person attic to a first-floor two-person room with a Minnesota native undergraduate. My housemates were full of energy and fun.

One fine spring day, the four students in the house decided to visit Como Park in St. Paul. l bought a six pack and some chips, and enjoyed the day. A policeman stopped the car, approached us with a smile, and asked who bought the beer. l said l did. He asked me, "Where are you from?"

l said, "Korea. We all are students at U. of M. enjoying the fine spring day."

The officer said, "l was there during the Korean War," and smiled.

l smiled and said, "Nice to meet you." l felt like l was meeting an old war buddy because l had served in the US Army as a civilian employee. Then he told me that in the United States minors were prohibited from drinking, unlike in Korea. The nice policeman left without giving me a ticket for my minor violation. In Korea, rice sake is often brewed at home, and at an early stage of fermentation, when the rice starch starts turning to sugar but before it turns to alcohol—rice sake is like Oriental soda with a slight hint of alcohol. In Korea we did not have a drinking age or "moonshine" violations at the time.

One day one of my classmates asked if l would like to go on a double date. l had no idea what that meant, but the word "date" sounded quite romantic, so I said yes. My classmate's date sat next to him, and my date and I sat in the backseat. I noticed my date had a silver wire across her front teeth, and I thought that must be a new tooth decoration among American girls.

During the 1958 summer quarter, I attended a special agricultural economic program at the University of Ohio sponsored by the Rockefeller Foundation for selected foreign students. After the summer program, we all went on a tour of Hoover Dam and the North Dakota Corn Palace, a huge structure built out of corncobs. The teenage tour guide asked me, "Who is the father of corn?" Of course, I did not know. She answered, "Popcorn!" We can always learn something from the younger folks.

We went to see Mount Rushmore, a masterpiece in terms of its size and the devotion and endurance of the builders. Then we visited an Indian reservation. One of the residents approached and greeted me with, "You are my cousin." He offered me the opportunity to stay with them for a few days, but I had to travel with the group and declined. Koreans originally drifted from the area of Mongolia, as some North American Indians likely did. Their physical features and customs resemble those of Koreans, including religious rituals, dancing, and totem poles.

Remittance from Korea was limited to $140 a month, and this was delayed due to Korean bank shutdowns. I discussed my predicament with my Korean classmate, Professor Park of Seoul University, who also depended on a fixed monthly stipend from the USAID–Seoul University funds. He offered me a hundred-dollar loan without any questions. I returned the loan a couple of months later with a box of chocolates for his little boy. This happened twice, and that was the last time I had to rely on personal loans from an individual. Professor Park earned his doctorate and went back to Seoul University as chair of the department and then moved on to serve President Park Jung-Hee as an economic advisor for eight years. I often visited him and his family when I went to Korea and talked about our times in Minnesota.

Between classes I started working at the university cafeteria three to four hours a day for $1.25 an hour. During the summer recess, I worked as a janitor for a seminary school with another American friend. The odd jobs gave me an education in American life and society and, best of all, introduced me to good friends.

In 1963 I was appointed assistant specialist in marketing in the Agricultural Extension Service of the University of Minnesota. I worked on writing "Minnesota Farm Business Notes" and US Department of Agriculture contract research. Once in a while, I tagged along with my boss, Professor Peterson, to give a talk to Minnesota farming communities on the market situation. Most of them were of Scandinavian descent and had never seen a Korean other than in the papers or in a movie.

I met my wife, Lois, while she was taking courses in the nurse anesthetist program in Minneapolis. She has been the director of nursing at a hospital in Fargo, North Dakota, and decided to become a nurse anesthetist. We married at Little Brown Church in the Vale in Iowa, where a long line of couples each paid ten dollars for a five-minute wedding ceremony. We both were going to school, so that was about the best wedding choice given our situation.

Lois loved the job of taking care of people, and everyone liked her. When she visited Korea for the first time in 1968, she loved to visit the traditional markets and countryside. When she went to the countryside, all the children would follow her around because most had never seen a woman with blond hair. She was from a farm and got a big kick out of a Korean farmer transporting two large pigs on the back of a small bicycle (I still have the photo).

At home in Virginia, Lois once invited about forty Korean embassy staff and their families for Scandinavian Thanksgiving dinner, even though she was working full-time at the hospital. She loved dogs and cats and antiques. She passed away in 2010. I miss her very much.

TEACHING AND GOVERNMENT SERVICE: UNITED STATES AND KOREA

I took my first job offer at the University of Georgia after completing my graduate program. In the summer of 1968, the USAID/USOM in Seoul asked me to come to Korea during the summer recess and teach research methods to government researchers and university professors. My project in Korea was nearly the last phase of the USAID program. Soon afterward, the USAID/USOM office closed down in Korea. Now Korea is helping other nations by sending out its missionaries and aid workers.

A former colleague at the University of Georgia took a job at the USDA in Washington, DC, and offered me a job as an economist. I moved to Washington after completing my USAID assignment in Korea in 1968.

My boss at the Economic Research Service, USDA, moved up into a newly formed Food and Nutrition Service, where food stamps and school lunch programs were planned and administered; he asked me to join him.

I left the US government job after fifteen years and went back to teaching in Korea in 1983, coinciding with Korea's boom in education and industry. I taught economics and initiated English language programs by hiring American, Canadian, and Australian staff at Kyungsung University in Busan. I also lectured as a visiting professor at Seoul National University and Korea University in Seoul. I served as a consultant to various Korean government agencies, and as a columnist for a Korean newspaper.

In 1998 I retired from teaching and returned to my home in northern Virginia. I sold my old Virginia home of forty years in 2012 and settled into a new home in Busan. It overlooks the Pacific Ocean, and I watch the sun rise in the morning and the moon rise at night. Reflecting on my experiences, I published two books in Korean, one is titled *The Unites States of America: Emulate the U.S. Selectively.*

Made in the USA
Charleston, SC
12 December 2014